This book belongs to

_____

This book is dedicated to my children - Mikey, Kobe, and Jojo.
Do unto others as you would have them do to you. - Matthew 7:12

Inclusive Ninja

By Mary Nhin

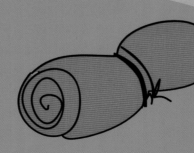

Pictures by
Jelena Stupar

No matter how different you were, Inclusive Ninja always made sure no one was being bullied or excluded. He had a way to make everyone feel included.

How did he learn this invaluable skill, you ask?

Well, we'd have to start from the beginning...

Once upon a time, there was a large crowd on the playground. One of the ninjas had dropped his hearing aid, and some of the ninjas chose to throw it back and forth.

Even though the ninjas were having fun,
Diversity Ninja felt that it was unkind.

Afterward, the ninja was trying not to let anyone see him crying.

You see, the other ninja who had dropped his hearing aid was Inclusive Ninja.

"It all begins with compassion," continued Diversity Ninja.

"To develop compassion, I pretend to be in the other person's shoes and feel what they are feeling by seeing the world through their eyes."

"Hmmm...I think I'm getting it," said Inclusive Ninja.

"Do you see that ninja with dark skin standing by himself? How do you think he feels?" asked Diversity Ninja.

"Do you see that ninja who's speaking another language? How do you think he feels?" asked Diversity Ninja.

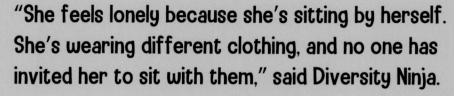

"She feels lonely because she's sitting by herself. She's wearing different clothing, and no one has invited her to sit with them," said Diversity Ninja.

"Some ninjas may have an accent, speak a different language, have another skin color, or own different beliefs," said Diversity Ninja.

"Some may not be able to walk or talk and may be limited in their abilities in some way."

"That doesn't make them weird, just different. And our differences make the world more interesting."

Inclusive Ninja decided from that day forward he was no longer going to be a witness, but an advocate of inclusion.

CAFETERIA

And that's how it came to be.

Wherever Inclusive Ninja was, you'd find compassion nearby.

Compassion and inclusion could be your secret
weapons against prejudice, racism, and bullying.

Fun, free printables at www.marynhin.com/ninja-printables.html

@marynhin @GrowGrit
#NinjaLifeHacks

Mary Nhin Grow Grit

Grow Grit